Small Talk

A Shy Introverts Guide to Being More Likeable and Building Better Relationships, Even If You Have Social Anxiety, Including Conversation Starters and Tips for Improving Your Social Skills

© Copyright 2019

All Rights Reserved. No part of this book may be reproduced in any form without permission in writing from the author. Reviewers may quote brief passages in reviews.

Disclaimer: No part of this publication may be reproduced or transmitted in any form or by any means, mechanical or electronic, including photocopying or recording, or by any information storage and retrieval system, or transmitted by email without permission in writing from the publisher.

While all attempts have been made to verify the information provided in this publication, neither the author nor the publisher assumes any responsibility for errors, omissions or contrary interpretations of the subject matter herein.

This book is for entertainment purposes only. The views expressed are those of the author alone, and should not be taken as expert instruction or commands. The reader is responsible for his or her own actions.

Adherence to all applicable laws and regulations, including international, federal, state and local laws governing professional licensing, business practices, advertising and all other aspects of doing business in the US, Canada, UK or any other jurisdiction is the sole responsibility of the purchaser or reader.

Neither the author nor the publisher assumes any responsibility or liability whatsoever on the behalf of the purchaser or reader of these materials. Any perceived slight of any individual or organization is purely unintentional.

Contents

INTRODUCTION 1

CHAPTER 1: WHAT IS SMALL TALK? 3

CHAPTER 2: UNDERSTANDING THE INTROVERT AND HOW THEY INTERACT WITH THE WORLD 8

CHAPTER 3: ARE THERE ANY ADVANTAGES TO BEING SHY? 15

CHAPTER 4: WHAT IS THE DIFFERENCE BETWEEN BEING SHY AND BEING AN INTROVERT? 21

CHAPTER 5: SOCIAL ANXIETY IS HOLDING YOU BACK AND HOW TO LEAVE IT IN THE DUST 25

CHAPTER 6: GOOD LISTENING SKILLS CAN MAKE SMALL TALK EASIER 31

CHAPTER 7: TIPS TO START A CONVERSATION AND KEEP IT GOING 39

CHAPTER 8: CAN I MAKE FRIENDS AS AN INTROVERT? 45

CHAPTER 9: SIMPLE THINGS YOU CAN DO TO BE MORE LIKEABLE 50

CHAPTER 10: HOW TO START AND BUILD UP RELATIONSHIPS AS AN INTROVERT 55

CHAPTER 11: OTHER WAYS TO INCREASE YOUR COMMUNICATION SKILLS 64

CHAPTER 12: TIPS TO HELP YOU DEVELOP YOUR SOCIAL SKILLS 74

CONCLUSION 82

Introduction

The following chapters will discuss what you need to know as an introvert, or someone who is shy, about starting small talk. As an introvert, you probably would rather spend your time at home, reading a book, watching a show, or doing another hobby that might not be considered "social". This is how you recharge your batteries and get a break from all the socialization that you get at work or at school.

But there are just some situations where you need to talk to other people, and the small talk that ensues can be difficult, and often brings you to a screeching halt with nothing to say.

This guidebook is going to help you deal with social conversations, and can make you an expert at small talk, no matter what your experience level was before. If you are a shy introvert, being able to hold a conversation and turn that simple small talk about unimportant topics into a deeper conversation later on is so important, and will help you to make the lasting friendships that you need and desire.

In this guidebook, we will look at a few different topics, especially about how introverts and shy people are two different personality traits (you can be shy without being an introvert, and not all introverts are shy), and how they view the world differently.

From there, we are going to explore valuable tips that will empower you to become great at small talk. We will look at how to become an active listener, rather than just thinking about what you will say next, how to be more likeable, and more.

There are so many instances in our lives when small talk can be important. And for a shy introvert, these times can prove to be a challenge. Most introverts would rather just stay home and not do too much socially. But they may still need to show up to events for family and friends, for work, or to make some new friendships. This guidebook will provide the tools needed to really get some great results with small talk, while still celebrating all the things that make an introvert unique!

Chapter 1: What is Small Talk?

Before we explore some tips that will help you improve your small talk skills, we first need to understand what small talk is. Small talk is a type of socially acceptable conversation that is essentially meaningless when it comes to its content, but it can serve an important function in certain situations and contexts.

For example, in many English-speaking countries, it is seen as unfriendly or rude for people not to participate in small talk. When you are looking for the right subjects to talk about with this kind of polite conversation, it is expected that you will stick with non-personal comments over non-controversial subjects.

Small talk is a way to be pleasant, for a few friends to catch up quickly, or just to pass the time when you are waiting for an event or in line, it is not the time to get into all of your political views or try to get a debate going. Keeping the conversation as light and breezy as possible is the key to ensuring that the small talk goes well.

A good example of small talk is discussing the weather. In fact, this is one topic that many of us already use on a daily basis when we run into people that we see only occasionally, or when we meet someone new. For example, you may find that as you chat with the cashier when getting your groceries that you talk about the weather, or a bit about your plans for the weekend.

Making conversation like this can sometimes be related to the situation at hand, such as waiting in a line. How many times have you been waiting in line at the store or at the post office and then started talking to someone nearby about how slowly the line is moving that day? You may use small talk and other forms of communication with those you see each day, but who you don't know very well. Another good example is a person that you run into in the halls of your apartment, but never really talk to for more than a few minutes.

Small talk can also be common at parties, such as when the guests all know the host, but they don't really know each other that well. During this time, it would be considered rude, and a little bit awkward, if no one mingled or talked to each other. So, each person will start getting together and talking about inconsequential subjects to help break the ice.

One way that this can be done—especially at a party—is with a compliment, such as one woman complimenting another on her dress. While compliments are acceptable, they also shouldn't make the other person uncomfortable, by referring to the person's body or sounding like a pick-up line. Guests who are at the buffet table could talk about the food that is offered, as they decide what to put on their plates to eat.

The point here is that small talk is not supposed to be very in depth. Since most small talk occurs between you and someone you don't know at all, or at least someone you don't know very well, you really don't want it to get much deeper than how long the line is taking or the weather recently. Keeping things light and airy is the point of small talk. The more general you can keep the topic, the better it is for everyone involved.

There are some people who love to use small talk. They may like to communicate in a verbal way with other people, or they may find the silence uncomfortable in some instances. There are others who like to meet new people and find that they really enjoy talking and learning more about them. Some people don't like this small talk at all, and often dread going out or going to a party because of it.

Every person deals with small talk differently. Some people find that they can meet up with anyone and form a connection with each person they come across. And then there are those who really struggle with small talk and maybe carry around a list of topics with them so that they can think of things when the conversation tends to lag a bit.

For many introverts, engaging in small talk is a challenge. They may already have a hard time talking to other people, especially those they don't know well. Perhaps they are already struggling with the venue or the situation they are in if it happens to be loud, new, or something that they don't particularly enjoy doing.

There are also some social constraints that happen with small talk, which can make it difficult to know what to say, putting further pressure on introverts who struggle with being out and around other people. Add to this that many introverts are shy, and small talk can be a pain. Just because someone is an introvert and needs quiet time alone, without being around people all the time, doesn't mean that they don't like people at all. They just need to take a different approach.

This guidebook will help with this. With some practice, and some time, even the shyest introvert will get better and they will see success. Anyone can learn how to use small talk to their advantage, they simply need to be ready to take some time to learn how to do it!

Based on the majority of the research that has been done on the topic, most people are happier, and experience a greater sense of well-being, when they are around other people. Being alone and in isolation for more than short amounts of time, even if you tend to prefer this, can be hard on the health. People who engage in conversations that are more meaningful, rather than just small talk, have a greater sense of wellbeing as well. But how do we build up to those deeper conversations? We need to start with small talk.

You usually don't end up in a deep and meaningful conversation with someone you just met. Instead, you start out with some basic small talk, and then, over time, you build up to the deeper conversations, the ones that are so good for your health.

If you are an introvert, or shy, or emotionally sensitive, small talk can be difficult, as this kind of conversation seems pointless and empty of meaning. However, it is unlikely that you can meet someone new, or even start a conversation with a friend, by just diving right in to any big issues that you have.

Always remember that for the most part, small talk is just the beginning of your connection with other people. It is going to be hard, and there will be times when you aren't going to want to do it. Maybe it feels the same as having to go out and get groceries and clean the house before you can have company over that you enjoy spending time with. The preparation is going to take work, and it is not going to be much fun. But once you have the company over and enjoy yourself, all that work seems worthwhile.

This is also true for meeting people and engaging in small talk. It is hard to do, and sometimes it doesn't always go the way that you would like. But after you have made a new friendship or a new connection with another person, you will find that the small talk was all worth it. You will feel good that you went out to a social event and made an effort.

When you work to build up your social skills with small talk, you will find that it becomes much easier to reach the deeper conversations and relationships that you desire.

Almost everyone runs into some trouble when they are working with small talk, and only a few people are naturally good at it. But if we want to be able to form deeper connections, friendships, and relationships that are so important to our wellbeing, we need to start somewhere, and that somewhere is with small talk. This guidebook is going to provide you with a lot of tips and tricks that you can use to get better at small talk, and to help you see the best results possible in no time.

Chapter 2: Understanding the Introvert and How They Interact with the World

Introversion and extroversion occur on a spectrum. What this means is that there are different stages or degrees of introversion, and no one person is completely an introvert or extrovert.

There are some innate qualities that many introverts share, including a love of introspection, a need for solitude, and a slower, more focused style of communication.

It is common for many introverts to feel overstimulated and drained by social interactions, and they may put up a wall around themselves to help them cope. When this happens, it may lead others to believe that an introvert is standoffish and cold, but most introverts are not actually this way.

Our society has a lot of myths about introverts. We have come to believe that being an introvert is a bad thing. The world values extroverts and assumes that everyone should strive to be that way.

And for those who fail, this can lead to them being looked down upon. But our world needs to be made up of both introverts and extroverts, and we can always learn from the opposite personality type.

Though each introvert is different, there are some common challenges and some common traits that they all share.

Introverts love to work with introspection

For an introvert, the idea of introspection comes naturally. Introverts love to explore their imagination, and all the colorful landscapes that exist there. Often, this inclination to daydream is criticized, and they may have been told at one point or another that they should stop and get their heads out of the clouds. The problem here is that there are some good reasons for introverts to be this way.

An introvert may feel like the outside world is an assaulting force—at every turn, once they leave their home, there are "energy vampires" that threaten to suck them dry. The introvert may turn inward as much as they can in order to feel a level of comfort, and to help them conserve their energy. This love of introspection also brings direction and meaning to their life.

Solitude is essential

Many introverts enjoy solitude, but this is often more than just a preference. In fact, this solitude is crucial for their happiness and health. Introverts need to have time during the day to be alone and recharge their batteries.

They may often feel pressure to get out of the house, usually from either well-meaning friends or those who just don't understand how an introvert functions.

If this pressure pushes the introvert to the point of being exhausted, they can become grouchy and irritable. They will then feel guilty for acting this way to their friends, and they may start to blame themselves for not being able to be "on" all the time.

If you are an introvert, it is important that you learn how to say "no", so that you can seek out the solitude that you not only crave, but also need, to survive. This will help your life to feel lighter. You can still go out, but you will also take the time to be alone and recharge, without guilt, which makes all of those social situations a lot more bearable. Even small talk will become easier to endure if you have been able to take a break and seek out solitude ahead of time.

The quiet introvert

Introverts are known for being quiet. While the rest of the world seems to praise extroverts who like to talk—seemingly just to hear themselves speak—introverts are generally quieter and will think more carefully before they talk.

An introvert's brain often works on the idea that less is more with conversations. Even though this is just the natural way that many introverts are, they may feel judged if they are asked, "Why are you so quiet?"

Studies have shown some big differences between the brain of an extrovert, and the brain of an introvert. One of the key differences between these two types of people is the way that information travels through the introvert's brain. Information takes a longer pathway and is processed more deeply, and this could be one reason why most introverts take longer to verbalize their thoughts.

Other characteristics of an introvert

> 1. Introverts are sometimes also highly sensitive in nature.
> 2. Introverts are often better at writing compared to speaking.
> 3. Introverts tend to prefer deeper conversations, rather than having to deal with small talk.
> 4. Introverts have a tendency to overthink things.
> 5. Introverts generally like to have structure in their lives, and to stay with their established daily structure.
> 6. Introverts have a rich inner life and are more likely to explore spirituality.

7. Introverts commonly dislike spending time talking on the phone.

The dilemma of most introverts

In our culture, extroversion is considered the norm. In fact, it is often seen as the superior personality type. But introverts really don't need to be transformed, fixed, or cured, so that they can be turned into extroverts—and this isn't possible anyway.

Extroverts are not superior, and neither are introverts. Both are completely different personality types at opposite ends of a spectrum, and they have different behaviors, desires, and needs from each other. This means that it is important for some understanding between the two groups, rather than pressure for the introvert to change.

Remember that there are also many different types of introverts. Some would rather spend the majority of their time at home and only go out on occasion. Others may find that they like to go out quite a bit, but they still need a break at times, so that they can replenish their energy.

Just because they are different from what is considered "normal", this doesn't mean that they should try to make themselves any different or try to turn into extroverts.

How an introvert sees the world

Introverts see the world in a different way than other personality types. They like to be at home, reading a book in comfort. They often prefer spending time with just a few close friends and family, over meeting new people and always being out. And even though they don't mind other people, they do usually prefer to work on their own.

Some other things that are important to note when it comes to understanding an introvert and how they interact with the world around them:

1. They are more likely to make themselves an expert in one thing, rather than a jack of all trades; introverts excel at focusing on a single skill or exercise until they master it. This allows them to shine at hobbies, such as playing a new instrument, painting, or performing magic tricks. It is far rarer to come across an introvert who has a more generic skill set. They like to focus on just one thing and master it, rather than trying to do a lot of different things.
2. They like to write to express themselves. An introvert is perfectly able to speak on a given subject, but they would rather use writing to put down all of their thoughts instead. You may find them with some paper and a pen, and they generally prefer to contact others with the use of emails and texts.
3. They really don't like to speak on the phone; the thought of a phone call that is planned can send some introverts into a meltdown. They can't stand this form of communication, and actively avoid it as much as possible. They try not to answer phone calls, unless they know that it is urgent, and will put off making calls until it is down to the last minute.
4. They think very carefully before writing or saying anything. No matter what kind of communication the introvert uses, they will be cautious and think through the points carefully before making them. This can mean that conversations will not be as fluid in their execution.
5. They like deeper conversations, but they do not like small talk. Discussions that are all about superficial matters can be hard and taxing emotionally for an introverted person. Instead, they will often choose to engage in conversations that have a deeper meaning and purpose. This is one of the reasons that some introverts aren't the best at meeting new people.
6. They like to look at the big picture, rather than jumping to conclusions. An introvert is someone who tries to look at both sides of the story, before they make any of their

decisions. They don't want to be too rash, and they want to make sure that they understand what is going on, and then make the right decision on the matter.

7. They will hold back when they are in a crowd. Introverts are more likely to find a small group of those they already know at a party, and then stick with them. But if they can't find anyone they know, an introvert will often speak to new people, though they may try to withdraw a bit and not communicate in the crowd.

8. They can succeed as a performer if they like, but they are not that fond of the limelight. Some introverts are good at performing, whether that is with acting, putting on a show, or just giving a presentation at work, but even if they do perform, they don't want the focus to be on them personally.

9. They often do their best work on their own. This may not be because they don't like other people, but because they prefer to just get the work done quickly, or in a certain way. Even when they are working alone, rather than as part of a team, they will get a lot of amazing work done, and usually they can get it done faster than others.

10. They are rarely bored, but they can get easily distracted. If you give an introvert a day at home alone, they will still be able to find many interesting ways to keep themselves busy and have fun. They might get lost in a book for hours, or find a room to clean or a game to play. Sometimes they have a hard time staying on track, but they will rarely ever be bored.

11. They are thorough and pay close attention to detail. This makes introverts valuable help in any situation where it is important that even tiny details are exact.

12. They are more drawn to being alone, and might pick out a somewhat solitary career path. Since introverts do so well working on their own, they will be drawn to a job where they can at least spend some of the time working individually on projects.

13. They will react differently to their surrounding environments. They may spend more time in their heads, and this means that things like sporting events, concerts, parties, and other social events won't give them the same rush that others experience.

14. When their energy is all gone, they are going to shut down. When an introvert has used up their energy reserves, they will close off and stop doing anything. They won't try to push through this exhaustion, and often they won't be able to find a second wind. Introverts don't seek out company to recharge their batteries, they just need to have some quiet time alone, without all the stimulation. It is better for them to recharge at home, where it is quiet and they don't have a lot of expectations put on them.

Just because someone is an introvert doesn't mean that they can't learn how to use small talk and get the benefits from it at the same time. An introvert may have to put some effort in to get better at small talk, and they may have to step out of their comfort zone a little bit to make it work. But if they can step out of that zone, they will be on their way to communicating better and making more friends in the process.

Chapter 3: Are There Any Advantages to Being Shy?

There are many people in our world who are considered shy, which means that they are nervous and timid around other people. Some people are incorrectly deemed as being shy because they are an introvert and they want to be left alone to recharge on occasion, rather than going out all the time. But others may be so shy that they share some of the same symptoms as those who are dealing with SAD or social anxiety disorder, but to a lesser degree. However, most people who are shy can learn to adapt to their surroundings and function in a world that is dominated more by the extroverts and outgoing personality types.

Many times, in our society, a shy person will be seen as abnormal or looked down on. Society has learned how to value extroverts who are outgoing and ready to be sociable all the time. While there is nothing wrong with being an extrovert, and our world needs them to function, there is also nothing wrong with being shy or being an introvert.

At the same time, someone who is shy may find that it is easy to get down on themselves because of this. It may seem like everyone around them is doing better socially, and they are going to be left behind.

At times like these, it is sometimes a good thing to consider the great advantages or benefits that come with being shy:

1. The modesty can be attractive.

You will find that most people who are shy are also modest. They are the last ones to announce their own accomplishments, and they might not even consider letting the world know what is amazing about them. They may even take this so far as shrinking away from any compliments or downplaying any of their own positive attributes.

Of course, you may find that having too much of this modesty eats away at your self-esteem, but a healthy dose can be a trait that is attractive to many. At the same time, as someone who is shy, you must be careful not to cross the line from modesty to self-deprecation. Some of the tips that you can use in order to make modesty work for you, and not let it go too far, include:

- Accept any compliments that others give you in a gracious manner.
- Recognize when you have achieved something important. Try to stay away from the idea of downplaying your successes and saying that they are just due to luck.
- Learn how to stand up for yourself if you ever feel that someone is taking advantage of you.
- Offer as much praise to others as you can. This can help you to understand what is of value and to accept praise yourself.
- Try to be as realistic as possible, rather than thinking that all things are bad, or all things are good.

2. Shy people will think before they act on something.

If you are already socially anxious, or at least just shy, then you are probably going to find ways to look before you leap into anything. This is a helpful trait to have when it is time to think critically about many important life decisions. Thinking carefully, and then planning things out before acting on them can be important when you are setting up goals for the long term; avoiding any unnecessary risks; or even when it comes to planning for the unexpected.

To support this theory, there was a study done in 2011 that compared the behavior of apes and human children. This study showed that human children would show more behavior in line with shyness compared to apes, and these children were less likely to approach something that was new. This could be used to suggest that humans may have developed the ability to look before they leap, so to speak, through this leaning towards being shy.

On the other hand, this tendency to think through things before taking any action needs to be moderated a bit. Thinking through where to work or what school to attend is a good thing. But thinking too long and hard about something that is meaningless, such as your lunch, can cause problems. If fear of taking a chance seems to be what is holding you back from some of your goals, then this means that you also need to learn to take a leap and just trust that things will work out well for you.

3. Shy people can seem more approachable.

Other people like to be around those who are shy because they don't act superior and this can often make it easier to talk with them. As long as it isn't too extreme, shyness, along with the self-effacing and modest nature that goes with it, is seen as non-threatening to others and can mean that they feel as comfortable as possible around you.

You need to be careful though because sometimes too much shyness can be misinterpreted and can make a person seem standoffish or aloof. If this is something that you are struggling with, you could start out slow. Start by saying something like: "Hello" and trying to smile at people so that you can show that you aren't really stuck up, you are just someone who is shy.

4. Shy people have a calming effect.

Sometimes shy people provide a calming influence to those around them, especially those individuals who are more highly strung. While shy people can deal with inner turmoil, their outward appearance is often calm, and they can seem like they are on an even keel emotionally. This calmness could end up having a positive effect on those who are around you.

However, if you feel that you are dealing with some inner turmoil, it is important to realize that it is fine for you to reach out to others for help. If your shyness means that you need to wear a mask all the time, see if you can start by opening up to one person about how you are feeling and see how much of a difference it makes for you.

5. Shyness can develop empathy.

Having a shy personality means that you are more likely to be an empathetic listener, which makes it much easier for others to open up and be honest with you. Having empathy for others makes you a compassionate friend, and it also suits certain careers. One of these positions could include a human services role, or any job where you need to help someone and there is one-on-one interaction.

6. Shy people tend to be more trustworthy.

We are always looking for those around us who are trustworthy. We want to find someone who will show up on time when they say they will. We want to find those who will help out or bring something if they promised they would. And we would like to be able to find someone who we can talk to, who wouldn't go and tell someone else and share our secrets.

Since a shy person isn't going to go around and toot their own horn, they aren't going to be the first ones who tell others about their own accomplishments. This also means that others are going to believe and trust them more. In some cases, this can even make a shy person into a better leader than an extrovert.

7. The ability to overcome many different things.

It is rare for someone to be really outgoing as a child and then become shy as an adult. Usually shyness is something that a person has had to struggle with their whole life. They have had to learn how to adapt to their surroundings while being shy, and to handle the difficulties that come when others don't understand why they behave in a certain way.

Since these people have struggled with shyness for so long, they really know what it is like to battle, endure, and overcome challenges. Without the struggle that they have gone through against shyness, they wouldn't have been able to develop the ability to cope with the different difficulties that come up in life.

8. Shy people often have deeper friendships.

Many times, a shy person will outwardly look like they are an introvert. However, shy people often do want to go out and socialize, but they are afraid to. They might not feel comfortable with small talk and would rather form some deep and meaningful connections with a few close friends. As a result, shy people spend time investing in a friendship with someone who understands who they are and why they are acting in a certain way, but it does take some time to develop.

Chances are that when a shy person does develop a friendship with someone, these friendships will be deep and long lasting.

9. Shy people can be dedicated employees.

There are a lot of jobs out there that will ask employees to focus and concentrate in a solitary role, and this an environment that shy people can flourish in. Not having a lot of social ties means that they will have fewer interruptions and less need to validate what they are doing in the eyes of others.

10. Shy people experience their rewards more fully than others.

There has been some research done that shows how the brains of shy people react more strongly to both positive and negative stimuli than others. What this means is that a shy person finds social situations more threatening compared to some of their outgoing friends, but that positive situations are also more rewarding. The increased amount of sensitivity to reward means that the shy person may find more value when it comes time to work towards their goals.

Having some daily shyness that isn't going to prevent you from participating in life and achieving your goals can have a lot of advantages. However, if the shyness becomes too severe and it starts to cause issues with the way you go about your day, this is not helpful, and you will need to work on improving. If you are already dealing with social anxiety or shyness that is severe, you should talk to your doctor and maybe seek the help of a mental health professional to get things straightened out.

Chapter 4: What is the Difference Between Being Shy and Being an Introvert?

Despite what a lot of people may think, being introverted and being shy are not the same. They may have a lot of similar characteristics, and on the surface, they can look the same, but they do have some big differences. An introvert enjoys spending their time alone, and they can sometimes feel drained emotionally if they spend a lot of time out with others. But a shy person doesn't enjoy being alone, they are just afraid to interact with those around them.

Let's consider two children who are in the same classroom. One of these children is shy and the other one is an introvert. When the teacher organizes an activity for all of the children in the class, the introverted child might prefer to stay at their desk and read a book because they find that spending time with the other children in the class can be stressful. But the shy child would really like to join in with the others, but they stay at their desk because they are scared to go over and join them.

Introversion is an intrinsic part of a child's personality and you won't be able to change or force them to act against their nature. But children who are shy can be helped to overcome this shyness. There are some introverts who are also shy, but this isn't true of all the introverts you meet. In fact, some of these introverts have excellent social skills, they simply choose not to interact all of the time because this leads them to feel drained, and they need to spend some time alone so that they can recharge their own emotional batteries.

While it is possible to use different techniques and even some therapy to help a person who is shy to overcome this obstacle, trying to turn an introvert into someone who is outgoing, or into an extrovert, will cause them a lot of stress and could make their self-esteem drop. Introverts are able to learn some different coping strategies that will make it easier for them to deal with a variety of social situations, but no matter what, they will always be an introvert.

Those who are dealing with shyness have a hard time when it comes to meeting and talking to someone new, and they don't like to find themselves in a brand-new situation. They might even feel so much fear about being in these situations, that they have physical symptoms, like blushing, shaking, sweating, and heart palpitations. It can sometimes be severe enough that it can cripple the individual and impact on their mental and physical health.

Of course, everyone can be shy in different types of environments, and there are a lot of different degrees when it comes to shyness. Most people are shy without having it turn into a problem and they will be able to use techniques to get over it.

Shyness and introversion are two personality traits that are often written down as the same thing by those who don't have to deal with both, one, or the other. Outgoing extroverts find it hard to see a big difference between these two personality types, and they just assume that all people who are shy are introverts, and all introverts are shy.

But this is not the case. It is possible for these two personality types to exist inside one person, but it is not a guarantee.

We have all been to one of those parties. There is that one person that is standing to the side, or maybe they are still within the group, but they look like they do not want to be there at all and are just waiting for the best chance to leave. In some cases, if you are an introvert, you are that person. Many people don't take the time to learn about these two personality types and how they differ, and they will brush it off, and this can get really grating on the individual, who feels like they are misunderstood.

One study that was done by the Salk Institute for Biological Sciences suggests that there is actually a different way that the introverted brain registers the world around them compared to others. When researchers took the time to study the activity in the brain of someone who is an introvert, it was found that the same amount of electrical activity occurred when they looked at an inanimate object and when they looked at another person.

This could really suggest another reason why a lot of introverts just don't want to look for social interaction. They not only get tired from doing it and feel a bit drained in the process, they may also find that this social interaction isn't stimulating to them at all, so they don't want to waste their time with it.

The introvert will go out on occasion. It isn't like they will never talk to others or that they avoid talking at all costs, and they do have friends as well. But they know their limits, and they know when they would rather be at home doing something else. And since introversion is more of a biological personality trait, most of those who are dealing with it are going to be completely fine heading home at the end of the day to be alone or spending their break time reading a book, instead of interacting.

While an introvert would choose to stay home on a Friday night because they don't see the interaction as stimulating, or they need to recharge their batteries after a long week, a person who is dealing with severe shyness may think that their only choice is to stay home, even though they wish that they could be out and about instead.

There are also some extreme cases where those who suffer from this kind of shyness will find that they can't function in many situations. For example, they may find that they can't ask for something as simple as directions from a stranger. Or, they may find that they aren't able to go to the front of a check-out line because then they will need to interact with another person.

Introverts are good at finding small groups of friends. When they have some people that they are close to, they can be great listeners, and they will provide thoughtful advice and be empathetic. But a person who is shy may find that it is more difficult to form the close friendships that they need. They may even feel awkward around people, including family and those that they have known all of their lives.

Introverts who are not also very shy can be fine if someone comes up to them and begins a new conversation out of the blue, even if the long conversation leaves them tired. But someone who is shy may find the thought of starting a new conversation—especially if they need to initiate it—terrifying.

The main difference between these two traits is how the person feels about the lack of social interaction and companionship. An introvert is fine with this. Even though others will assume that they aren't okay and will try to convince them to go out, the introvert is usually happy with the results that they have. But for someone who is dealing with shyness, they tend to wish that they could go out and have more friends. They are the ones that feel there is something holding them back and they just aren't able to put themselves into the situations that would make this possible.

Chapter 5: Social Anxiety is Holding You Back and How to Leave It in the Dust

Social anxiety is the fear of feeling negatively judged by those around you, which can lead you to feel inferior, depressed, humiliated, embarrassed, and inadequate. If you become irrationally anxious in social situations and think that you will be much better off alone, then you may be dealing with social anxiety.

Social Anxiety Disorder (SAD), which used to go by the name of social phobia, is a much bigger problem than researchers initially thought. It is now estimated that millions of people throughout the world are dealing with anxiety each day, whether they are experiencing one of the specific forms of the condition, or just generalized social anxiety.

In the epidemiological studies done in the United States, Social Anxiety Disorder was found to be the third largest psychological disorder in the country, and only after disorders like alcoholism and depression. In fact, it is estimated that around seven percent of the population of the United States suffers from some form of social anxiety right now, but the lifetime prevalence rate for developing this kind of disorder is somewhere between thirteen to fourteen percent.

Of course, these are just estimates and there could be many more people who suffer from social anxiety that either don't realize it, or don't seek help for the condition. These numbers are just based on those who have gotten help because they already knew that they were dealing with social anxiety in their lives. In any case, the numbers are high and show how prevalent this problem can be.

Social anxiety can manifest in many ways, and one example that affects many people, even on a small scale, is the fear of speaking in front of groups. Those with more generalized social anxiety feel uncomfortable, nervous, and extremely anxious, no matter what kind of social situation they are dealing with at the time.

When things like anticipatory anxiety about being in social situations, feelings of being inferior, embarrassment, depression, indecision, worry, and self-blame are present no matter what kind of life situation you are in, then this is generalized social anxiety at work.

The symptoms of social anxiety disorder

There are numerous symptoms that can show up when it comes to suffering from social anxiety disorder. People who are dealing with this kind of disorder often experience a significant amount of emotional distress when they are in a variety of situations, including:

    1. Any interpersonal relationships, whether they are romantic in nature, or friendships.
    2. When participating in group activities, and they know that they will need to say something.
    3. Most social encounters, but especially when going to meet up with strangers.

4. Meeting people who are in a position of authority, or who are considered "important" people.

5. While being observed as they complete a task.

6. If they are the center of attention, no matter what the reason is.

7. If they feel they are being criticized.

8. Being introduced to someone new.

Of course, these aren't all the symptoms that you could face. The physiological manifestations that come with Social Anxiety Disorder can also include things like muscle twitches of the neck and face, trembling, difficulty swallowing, dry throat and mouth, excessive sweating, turning red or blushing, a racing heart, and an intense fear of what is going to happen next.

Those who are dealing with Social Anxiety Disorder already know the anxiety that they feel is extreme, and that it really doesn't make any sense. Even though these individuals are facing their fears each day when they leave the house, their feelings of anxiety persist and show no signs of easing.

Treating social anxiety

It is not always easy to seek the help that is needed to treat any mental health issue, whether it is Social Anxiety Disorder or another condition. If you are already reluctant to talk to strangers, or other people in your life, then how are you supposed to ask for help? If you have let this anxiety go on for too long and you are now at the point where you are avoiding any social contact, or it has started to control your life, then it may be time to talk to a mental health professional.

It is never a good idea to let this social anxiety go on unchecked. If you become scared to deal with other people, or to get into any kind of social situation like eating in restaurants, public speaking, dating, or attending parties, then this could signify a problem. When you start to cut yourself off because of social anxiety, you may develop low self-esteem or feel depressed.

The first thing that you need to do is make an appointment with your doctor. There are a few ways that the doctor may determine if you have social anxiety, including:

> 1. A physical exam. This helps to assess whether there is any medical condition that you have, or if you take any medications that can trigger these symptoms of anxiety.
> 2. By discussing your symptoms and how often these symptoms occur and in what situations.
> 3. By reviewing a list of many different situations to see if these seem to make you anxious.
> 4. Asking you to self-report on questionnaires about the symptoms of social anxiety and see if you match up.
> 5. If you meet the criteria that is listed in the Diagnostic and Statistical Manual of Mental Disorders. This is something that is published by the American Psychiatric Association.

There are a few different types of treatments that your doctor may choose to prescribe. Since just facing your fear won't do much on its own, and often makes the situation worse, the doctor is likely to offer a few other options. Treatment will depend on how much this anxiety is affecting your ability to function in your daily life. Some options that you can usually investigate include talk therapy or psychotherapy, medications, or both.

First, let's explore psychotherapy. In therapy, you are going to learn how to recognize and then change the negative thoughts that you are having about yourself. You can then move on to developing skills that will make it easier to gain confidence in all social situations.

There are a few options available for this, but cognitive behavioral therapy (CBT) is considered the most effective when it comes to anxiety. This type of therapy can be successful whether it is done in a group or individually.

When dealing with exposure-based cognitive behavioral therapy, the patient is gradually exposed to situations that they fear the most. This can make it easier for individuals to improve their coping skills and can help them to deal with any situations that induce anxiety. Another way to do this is to participate in skills training or role playing to practice social skills and gain some confidence and comfort. Practicing this kind of exposure to social situations can be a good way to help challenge any worries that you have.

There are also a few different types of medication that can help deal with this kind of anxiety. One common option is selective serotonin reuptake inhibitors (SSRIs). It's thought that these have a good influence on things like mood by boosting serotonin levels in your brain. Your doctor may otherwise suggest that you need to take some medications like Zoloft or Paxil depending on how severe the anxiety is.

Of course, the need for medication needs to be weighed against any possible side effects. Since many of these medications might cause a lot of side effects, the doctor could start you out with a low dose first to see how you handle it. You will then need to follow up a few times to help adjust the medication to the dosages that you need. It could take you up to a few months of treatment with a particular medication before you notice an improvement to your symptoms.

Some of the other medications that your doctor could prescribe to you to help with social anxiety and its symptoms, include:

   1. Antidepressants. You may have to work with a few different options in order to see if they work for you. There are many different types of antidepressants, and they all have a variety of side effects. The therapist or your doctor will most likely want to try them out to see what works the best, with the fewest side effects, for you.
   2. Anti-anxiety medications. Some medications known as benzodiazepines help to reduce how much anxiety is felt in some individuals. They can work very fast, and you may notice a change in the symptoms quickly. However, these are strong and tend to be habit forming and sedating so if you are prescribed these, it is going to just be for the short term.

3. Beta blockers. These are medications that will try to block some of the stimulating effects that come with adrenaline. These can help to reduce symptoms like shaking voice and limbs, pounding of the heart, blood pressure, and heart rate. They can be used on an infrequent basis to help you control your physical symptoms in some situations that may bring up your anxiety.

It is important to remember that any treatment for Social Anxiety Disorder isn't always going to work quickly. You can continue to work with therapy and take medication for many months to help you out. The symptoms can fade over time, and often after you build up some confidence with the way things are going, you will be able to discontinue the medication. To help you make the most of your treatment, try to attend all of your appointments for therapy, challenge yourself by picking out goals and pursuing them, and take any medications as directed.

Chapter 6: Good Listening Skills Can Make Small Talk Easier

Small talk can be a lot of work for many people who don't like trying to think about inconsequential topics to keep the conversation going. They may be uncomfortable with getting the other person to start talking, and they want to make sure that they don't say anything that is going to offend the other person or to cause a big lull in the conversation.

One of the keys that you can work on to make sure that you can get small talk to work well, is to listen. The more that you can listen and gather from the other person, the easier it is to keep the conversation flowing.

Here are some of the key skills that you need to use in order to practice active listening, so that small talk will be more effective for you:

Don't do all the talking

It is common to get nervous when talking to others. To avoid any silence when the conversation comes to a stop, we may overcompensate and start to talk aimlessly, barely letting the other person talk at all.

If you don't pause to allow a natural back-and-forth, then you risk turning the conversation into a monologue. The good news about active listening is that you don't have to talk too much, as you encourage the other person to do most of the talking.

This doesn't mean that you should just stand there and say nothing the whole time. But if you use active listening to bring up the right questions, you may be able to keep the conversation going for quite some time, without really having to do much talking at all.

For example, you can ask more questions about the topic at hand; you can ask for clarification; and then you can ask a few more questions to bring the conversation back up again when needed. Talking is important but try to get the other person to do a lot of talking, while you listen, as much as possible.

Try to put the speaker at ease

When you start small talk with a new person, whether you have met them before or it is the first time that you have ever spoken to them, try to put them at ease as quickly as possible. It is natural for both you and for them to be a bit nervous by the situation, but if you are able to put the other person at ease, then you are going to feel more at ease as well.

Your job here is to try to help the other person feel like they are open and free to speak about anything that they want. Remember their concerns and needs, and listen to what they have to say. Make sure that you use nods or other gestures and words to encourage the other person to continue with what they are saying, and to show that you are truly interested.

Eye contact can be so important here. Do not look at the floor, look at your hands, or look at other things that are going on around you. This is going to send out the wrong message, and makes the other person feel like you are bored with them, or that there are more important things for you to focus your attention on.

Strong eye contact, without staring and seeming aggressive, is so important. You need to look the other person in the eyes, while smiling and appearing attentive, to show that what they have to say is important and you are listening, understanding, and appreciating the conversation.

Find ways to remove distractions

There are always going to be a lot of distractions that show up in the world around you. Whether it is from your phone beeping, from others walking around, and even from your email. But if you let yourself get distracted by all these things, then your attention is taken away from the conversation at hand. How are you supposed to be effective at engaging in small talk, or any kind of communication, if you are so distracted that you can't even hear what the other person is saying?

When you are working on your listening skills, make sure that all the distractions are put away. Turn off the computer, the phone, and the television, to make sure that there is no chance that they will get in the middle of the conversation. Don't look out the window, pick at your fingers, shuffle papers, or doodle. This kind of distracted behavior sends a message to the other person that you are bored or disinterested in them and what they have to say. If your roles were reversed, how would that make you feel?

If you can, it is also important to avoid any interruptions. While you may not be able to avoid these all the time—for example, if you are at a party and someone walks over and interrupts, there isn't much you can do—you can try to avoid them as much as possible.

You want to make sure that you can put your full attention on the speaker, and that you make them feel at ease and like the most important person around. You can't do that if you are constantly checking your email on your phone, looking out the window, or looking around the room.

Empathize

Empathy is one of your strongest tools in communicating and forming meaningful connections with others. It is easy to come off as thoughtless or insensitive if your ability to experience and express empathy isn't well developed. When you are talking to someone, try to understand how they are feeling from their point of view. Even if what they are experiencing and talking about isn't something that you have gone through personally, and even if it isn't something that you understand all that well, it is still important to find some common ground and then use that to help you to empathize with the other person.

For example, if you find that you don't respond much if another person is obviously feeling very happy or sad, or if you give harsh, tone deaf responses to a friend whose dog has died—because they should have "expected" it, since dogs don't live as long as humans, then you might need to work on developing your emotional empathy.

It is also important to develop cognitive empathy, which involves trying to understand how someone is feeling from a more logical perspective. For example, if you get annoyed at someone else who is not as educated as you, simply because they don't know something that you think should be "obvious", you need to work on improving your cognitive empathy, and understanding that not everyone has had the same opportunities as you to advance their studies.

If possible, let go of any preconceived notions that you have about a person. When you start out the conversation with an open mind, it is easier to have some empathy with the speaker and to respond appropriately. Reading widely and on a wide range of topics is another great way to expose yourself to many different viewpoints and life experiences. Not everyone has the same reaction to events as you do, and it's important to recognize this and to try and learn about someone else's viewpoint, which can help to develop your empathy.

Of course, there may be times when the other person is going to talk about a topic, or say something, that you don't really agree with.

This doesn't give you the right to just barge in and start talking over them or putting them down for their perspective. Instead, if you do disagree with that person, you can wait and construct an argument later that will respectfully respond to what they said.

Even if you do decide to counter what the speaker has said because you don't agree with them, this doesn't mean that you should close your mind and ignore their feelings. When it comes to any kind of communication, whether it is in the form of small talk or not, it is so important to keep an open mind to the opinions, emotions and views of others. Even if you don't end up agreeing with them completely, you may be able to learn a few things along the way.

Don't interrupt with your own solutions

We are taught as children not to interrupt other people when they are talking. But much of what we see on television and in popular culture shows that it is just fine to interrupt someone and put in your own solutions.

Interrupting is one of the worst things that you can do when trying to have a conversation, whether you are talking to someone you just met, or someone you have known for a long time. When you interrupt, it is sending the message that:

> 1. This isn't a conversation. I see it as a contest, and I plan to win it.
> 2. I don't have time to wait around for your opinion.
> 3. I don't really care what you think, but I think that you should listen to me.
> 4. What I have to say is way more relevant, accurate, or interesting compared to what you have to say.
> 5. I'm more important than you.

Each person thinks and speaks at different rates. If you are already a quick thinker, and an agile talker, then it is going to be a burden for you to relax your pace if you come across a communicator who is thoughtful and a bit slower to express themselves.

Making an effort not to interrupt the other person helps to keep the conversation at an even pace and to ensure that you actually hear what the other person is saying, rather than talking over them.

Any time that you are listening to someone talk about one of their problems or another issue affecting them, you should work hard to not just suggest solutions. Most people aren't really looking for advice because they just want to be able to talk and let off some steam. If they do want some solutions, they are going to specifically ask for it. You need to listen and help the other person find their own answers. Somewhere down the line, if you are absolutely bursting with a great solution, at least ask the other person whether they would like to hear the idea first.

Wait until the speaker pauses before asking for any clarifications

When you don't really understand what someone is saying, it is fine to ask them questions to make sure that you understand what is going on. It is much better to ask them to backtrack or to ask some questions to make sure you fully understand what is going on, rather than just continuing the conversation and being confused the whole time.

But make sure that you don't interrupt the other person when you ask for clarification. Wait until there is a natural pause from the speaker. Then, you can ask something like: "Back up a second. I didn't understand what you just said about..." This allows you a chance to get clarification, but it also shows the other person that you were listening to them and that you really want to hear what they have to say.

Ask questions but stick to the topic

During a conversation, there may be many points that come up that can lead to a conversational tangent that gets things off track. For example, at lunch, a colleague starts telling you about their recent trip overseas. In the course of this talk, they mention visiting a mutual friend. This can lead you to ask questions about that one mutual friend, and soon the topic has moved off from the original discussion about all of the amazing places that your colleague saw on holiday.

There is nothing wrong with asking questions to explore different elements of a topic—in fact, this can often help a conversation to evolve and flow well—but try to keep things relevant and on the same topic that the other person wants, at least to start with. If you notice that the question you have asked is leading the speaker astray, then you should take the responsibility to get it back on track. This can make the person you are talking to feel like they still have control over the conversation, and it helps you to practice going with the flow.

Pay attention to some of the nonverbal cues

There is a lot that the other person can say with their words, but there is even more that the other person can say that is nonverbal. It is possible to glean a lot of information from another person without them even saying a word. This can even happen over the phone, with the help of listening to the inflections in their voice.

There are a lot of different nonverbal cues that you can pay attention to, when it comes to having a face to face conversation with another person. You can see whether the other person is irritated, bored, or enthusiastic just by observing their body language, the sound of their voice, and the expression on their face. These are all clues that you shouldn't ignore.

When you are listening to someone else and trying to glean everything that they want to tell you, you must be careful of what else is being said below the surface of their words. What the other person is saying out loud will only convey a fraction of the message. The nonverbal cues are just as important.

Show some regular feedback to the speaker

When trying to connect with another person during a conversation, it is important to give regular feedback. If you just stand there passively looking like a blank slate, not responding to them in any way, it will make the other person feel as if they aren't getting through to you and they will start withdrawing from you.

It can help to mirror their posture and body language, for example. You can also show the speaker that you understand where they are coming from by saying things like: "I can see that you are confused", "What a terrible ordeal for you", or: "You must be thrilled" in response to their story. If you are talking to that person and you find their thoughts and feelings unclear, then you can simply go through and paraphrase the message, as you understand it, on an occasional basis.

From there, you can just nod and show that you understand them with the help of appropriate facial expressions. The idea here is to give the speaker proof on some level that you are listening and that you are still following along with them on their train of thought.

You need to be an active listener when you are using small talk. Too many times we get involved in our own thought processes and expectations about how a conversation should unfold, instead of letting it flow and evolve naturally. If two people meet who are doing the same thing, then the conversation will come to an awkward halt.

But when you become an active listener, you will find that you can learn so much. You can easily catch on to the topics that the other person is bringing up, you can understand and respond to the cues that they send, and ask interesting questions to propel the conversation. You can feed off that and keep the conversation going for much longer, without feeling worn out, worried, or strained to find more topics to discuss.

Chapter 7: Tips to Start a Conversation and Keep It Going

Not knowing how to keep a conversation going can really harm your social life. Awkward silences can be uncomfortable for everyone, but the good news is that there are different things that you can do to get around them.

For many people, one of the most daunting things about meeting strangers or trying to make new friends is the risk of not knowing what to say. But if you do know how to start and keep a conversation going, it can make socializing much more enjoyable, and help you to create some lasting friendships.

Why do I run out of things to say?

One habit that gets in the way of a dynamic, flowing conversation, is filtering. This is the process of holding yourself back from saying something out loud, until you have had a chance to filter it first. This supposedly allows you to make sure that the sentence you are about to say is interesting, smart, impressive, or cool, and that it won't embarrass you.

While this approach may make sense in your head, it is effectively killing your conversation ability.

Another problem that can come up is not learning how to get in the mood to start a new conversation. For example, if you just spent a whole day studying or analyzing intense subjects, you might find it quite hard to switch off from thinking about these topics, before you are ready to talk and interact with people on a social level.

How do you overcome this issue? You can overcome it in a simple way by learning some new skills to get yourself in the right mindset to associate with others socially. Here are some tips and important points to consider, so that you never run out of things to say again. Once you can do this, you will find that it is much easier to talk with people and make new friends.

How can I keep a conversation going?

There are a few different skills that you can develop to help keep a conversation flowing.

1. No filtering.

The first thing is to stop filtering yourself all the time. You are only hindering your own confidence if you keep stopping yourself from saying what is on your mind, with thoughts like: "Would I sound stupid if I say this?"

The best way for you to practice speaking more freely is to start with people that you know at least a little bit. It is sometimes fun to find out that you can say whatever comes mind during a conversation, and as long as it isn't widely inappropriate, no one is going to judge you for sharing your thoughts. People aren't really that interested in whether or not what you have said is "cool" enough. They are too focused on trying to keep the conversation going and on how they come across to you, so just talking and being yourself by bringing up any subject that comes into your head can make a big difference.

2. "Interesting, tell me more!"

This is an approach that can work a good ninety-nine percent of the time, and it is a surefire technique that beginners really like to work with. People love to know that you are truly interested in what they are telling you. If you can show them a bit of genuine interest, it is more likely that the person you are talking to is going to hang around longer. This is a great way to keep a conversation going without much effort on your part.

There are some variations of this phrase that will also encourage the speaker to keep on talking, such as asking follow-up questions in response to what has been said.

When the other person sees that you are actively listening and interested, it will help put them at ease and they are going to be more engaged and willing to share information with you.

3. Stories can come from everywhere.

A good story can get everyone involved and keep a conversation going with ease. You don't have to exclusively draw from the experiences in your own life when you are starting a conversation. It is perfectly fine to use stories that didn't happen to you personally, to help keep the conversation going. For example, you can talk about something that your friend told you; an anecdote that you heard on TV; or even what you read in the news.

This technique is a great way to make any conversation that you are having more interesting, with more of a natural ease, avoiding all the silences that can show up and make things more awkward.

Additional tips to enhance your conversations

Some other ideas that will help the conversation go smoothly when using small talk, include:

- Be interested in what they have to say. You need to find ways to be really interested in the conversations that you have with other people. If you don't seem interested, whether or not you are is irrelevant, because the other person will get

bored or frustrated and will walk away from the conversation in no time.
- Ask lots of questions. When the other person brings up a new topic, start to ask questions about it. This shows that you want to learn more, and it will do wonders to keep the conversation going. It can also work well if you don't know the topic that the other person brings up, because then you can participate and learn along the way.
- Be good at listening. If you let your mind wander too much and don't really listen and pay attention to what the other person is saying, it is hard to take in what they tell you. You have to make sure that you can take in all of the information that they provide you, instead of going around in an endless loop of questions because you weren't really giving it the attention that it needed.
- Make eye contact. Maintaining respectful eye contact is another way to let the other person in the conversation know that you are listening to them. If you are constantly moving your eyes around, then you are going to appear distracted and like you are not that interested in what the person is saying.
- Consider keeping a list of topics to hand. Sometimes it is hard to think of topics when you are meeting with someone new, and you may feel some anxiety about this. If the conversation is already moving and flowing along, you may not even need the list, but having it in the back of your mind just in case the conversation starts to lag, can take some of the pressure off.
- Find some common ground. When you find something that you and the other person have in common, you may want to try and stretch that thread into a longer conversation. You can pay attention to find some common ground during the discussion, or you might be introduced by someone who already knows what mutual interests the two of you share.

- Use conversation "threading". This is where you pick up on multiple points of interest in a statement made by another person. You can then ask various questions to branch off the conversation, for example, if someone says: "Last week, I traveled to Alaska for work", you could ask if they like to travel in general and discuss some of your own stories about traveling. You could also ask them where they are working, or what they thought about Alaska. This opens a lot of doors, as you can naturally direct the way you would like the conversation to go.
- Practice and get out there. The more that you can practice small talk, the easier it will be. You can practice conversing with anyone around you, whether it is someone at the grocery store, a family member, or a friend. You can even try if you are online in a video chat. Over time, this will make small talk feel so much more natural and will help to build your confidence.
- Know when it is time to put an end to the conversation. This is a very important part to consider for any conversation. If things are going well, then it is hard to figure out when to end things. You don't want to interrupt the other person, but you do want to make sure you leave before the connection runs out. It is easier to end too early, and leave them wanting more, than to talk with them for too long and have either of you get bored. When you are ready to end the discussion, make sure to let the other person know that you would like a chance to talk with them later, and then share contact information so that this is possible.

Now that you know some of the tricks that you can use to ensure your conversations don't stall, the next thing that you need to do is practice using these techniques. The best way to practice is to get out there and use them the next time that you talk to someone new.

Of course, if you have been struggling with the issue of small talk for some time, it is a good idea to start by implementing just one of these ideas at a time, and find a way to add your own twist to it, so you aren't overwhelmed. From there, you will be able to slowly implement these tips and engage in some of the best conversations of your life.

Chapter 8: Can I Make Friends as an Introvert?

When you are an introvert, you may find that it is hard to make friends. It isn't that you don't want to make friends or that you don't like people. But in a world where extroverts—who enjoy being sociable and who expect you to be the same—are everywhere, while you want to be at home relaxing to recharge your batteries, it can be really hard.

This doesn't mean that all is lost if you are an introvert. Introverts can be some of the best types of friends to have, and you will be able to find those who want to spend time with you and won't ask you to change your personality to be with them. But you may have to take a few extra steps in order to make this happen. There are some things that you can do as an introvert to start making more friends and enjoying your social life a little bit more than before.

The challenges of making friends when you are an introvert

There are many challenges that can impact your ability to make friends when you are an introvert. A lot of social situations that include small talk can be hard, and when you are perfectly content to spend a lot of time at home with a good show or reading a good book, it can be difficult to drag yourself away to go be social and do things that physically drain you.

Some of the different challenges that can come in to play when you are trying to make friends as an introvert include:

1. Maintaining too many friends and having too many types of friendships can be overwhelming. As an introvert, you may worry that others will not be willing to put up with your tendency to go off the radar on occasion and take a break.

2. Getting into a group and dealing with a group conversation is intimidating. You are never quite sure when to interject, or how to express yourself without feeling like there is a big spotlight put right on you.

3. In some cases, you can feel a bit of frustration when there is a conversation that goes too fast, and you are not able to fully think about the topic and give your opinion.

4. Small talk is often tedious, or even painful, for a shy introvert. They will sometimes find it difficult to smoothly bridge the gap between deeper conversations and chit chat.

5. Many of the social environments that are needed in order to make friends can be overwhelming to an introvert, and when they do venture out, it can leave them unmotivated to get out there and try it again.

In addition, there are going to be some generic challenges that all adults face when it is time to make friends, even for those who are considered extroverts. Adults tend to be less open to forming new friendships as they get older. They tend to be settled into their own friend groups that they have formed over the years, and it is sometimes hard to break into one of these if you don't already have your own group.

If you have ever gone through the experience of moving churches, cities, or jobs, you know that it is tough to break into some of the friend circles that are already there. As an introvert, you may find that instead of breaking into the whole group and gaining a ton of friends, it can be preferable to have just a few best friends you can rely on, ones who feel like home and will be there for you.

Sometimes you just need one

There is often a misconception out there that you have to juggle a ton of friends, and a non-stop social activity calendar, in order to feel like you are living a good life. Instead of trying to get out of your comfort zone too much, it is often best if you can just find a few people to make a tight-knit friend circle.

Introverts are not hardwired to always be out in social activities, and to maintain a lot of shallow friendships. Instead, they value quality over quantity with all of their relationships. This isn't meant to discourage you from making friends, and if you decide to have a bigger group of friends, that is entirely possible to achieve.

The good news is there are a few things that you can do to help you make friends as an introvert. These include:

Frequent a "friendship goldmine"

Mining a "friendship goldmine" involves participating in any kind of activity that you would naturally plan on doing, regardless of whether you were trying to make friends doing that activity or not. This is something that you can usually tie to a passion, a core value, or a higher goal of yours, like dancing, attending church, or taking French lessons. This is a great idea because you will take the pressure off as you do an activity you enjoy, and you will hopefully also find friends who have the same hobbies, goals, and passions as you.

You can choose to take a pottery class, or go to an exercise group, or spend time in a book club—the possibilities are endless. And you will be able to go to these activities for some time and will see those new people on a regular basis.

This no-pressure approach will help you to get to know someone new, while doing something that you love. If you make new friends at it, that is great, and you can carry those friendships forward into your daily life. But if you don't make a new friend, you can try out something else later, and at least you got to do something that you already enjoy or always wanted to try.

Let things be a little awkward

No one likes to end up in situations that are overly awkward. But when you are a shy introvert who is trying to make some new friends, this is something that is going to happen on occasion. The thing to remember here is that the awkward part is only going to last for the first few minutes. If you are able to accept and even expect this discomfort in the beginning, you will find that this passes quickly and you can often still connect well afterwards.

Once you can power through those few minutes, you will start to form some of the connections that you need. And if the other person isn't able to handle those few minutes of discomfort and decides to move on to talking to someone else, then they weren't the friend for you.

Set realistic friendship goals

The reason that a lot of introverts get discouraged so quickly when they are dating or trying to make new friends is because they hope that they will connect with someone after only one or two outings. If we start to expect that every social event is going to provide us with some friends for the rest of our lives, we will feel very discouraged early on.

The goals that you set for coming up with these new connections need to be more achievable. Realistically, it could take quite a few meetings and social events, spread over a longer period of time so you recharge as needed, before you make any new lifelong friends. In some cases, it may just take one or two interactions to set this solid foundation, but that shouldn't be your goal.

Some of the reasonable goals that you can set yourself include:

> 1. Initiating a conversation with one or two new people each time that you are at a social event.
> 2. Practicing one of the tips that we are talking about in this chapter, such as starting a regular activity that you enjoy, like

pottery classes, and see if you make any connections as the classes unfold.

3. Smiling, in a genuine manner, at a minimum of two or three people when you go out.

If you are able to aim for some of these micro goals, you will find that it is much easier to stay optimistic and motivated when working to make some new friends.

This may seem like a lot to handle—but making friends as an introvert doesn't always have to be a big challenge. If you can take things slowly and really work towards your goals, while making those goals manageable for your personality type, you will be amazed at the results.

Chapter 9: Simple Things You Can Do to Be More Likeable

Are you someone who wants to be able to increase how likable you are? Would you be interested in starting up a conversation with anyone you meet and have them like you instantly?

Everyone wants to make sure that they are liked. Some people care about this more than others, but it is a natural human instinct—we are hardwired to want to fit in and "belong". It makes us uncomfortable or upset to hear that someone doesn't like us, even if we don't know that person all that well.

There are some people who naturally have a personality that makes them more likeable. They know what to say to others, how to act, and how to make other people feel good. Even if you don't have these skills, there are some simple steps that you can follow in order to improve your congeniality to become someone that others are interested in and like as well.

Learn how to treat people better

It's important to make sure that we know the proper way to treat others. To do this, start with a smile. This is a great and simple way to get the attention of another person. Smiling, if it is done in a natural way that doesn't look forced, shows that you are friendly and approachable, and that you are a positive person. Any time that you can, always come prepared with a natural smile. A fake smile can work as well, as long as it doesn't look too forced in the process.

A smile is one of the friendliest greetings out there, and it can work to instantly put people at ease. If you want to start up a conversation with someone else, or you see someone else that you recognize, you should stop for a minute and flash them a smile. This is usually going to make them feel good and can encourage them to like you more.

You should also focus on your body language and the message that you are sending out, to make sure that you are approachable. If you are at an event and you stand back against the wall, keeping your arms crossed with a pout on your face, you will appear to others as unfriendly and annoyed. This will make them think that they should just stay away from you.

Your body language is going to be so important when it comes to showing that you are approachable and that you want to talk to other people. Welcoming others, smiling, and standing with good posture and your arms uncrossed at your sides, can really go a long way in making others feel more comfortable around you.

You may also find that steady eye contact can be a good touch as well. Just make sure that your eye contact is not too intense, and that you remember to blink occasionally so that you don't end up intimidating the other person in the process.

We also need to focus on the importance of being kind. It is sometimes difficult to reach out to everyone you come across with an attitude that is pleasant, particularly if you are feeling drained or annoyed. But if you can do this with as many people as possible, it can go a long way to building up your good reputation. Research has also shown that there are some reward centers of the brain that are more activated if we act generously, like when we help a friend or donate to a charity. Not only does being kind help others to feel good, it will show that you are a caring person, and can also be a good thing when it comes to your own happiness and health.

The way that you make people feel is one of the main things that they will remember about you. Make sure to show respect and try to be polite, for example by holding open the door for others, shaking hands with those that you meet, and treating others the way that you would like to be treated. If you are actually in the wrong for something along the way, make sure that you apologize and act humble in the process.

When you are meeting someone for the first time, a good impression that you can leave with them is remembering their name. Whether it is someone you see at the store on a regular basis, or a business contact, learning the names of these people can be so important and will really make them feel valued and warm towards you in your future interactions. It is easy to forget an acquaintance's name, and just by remembering it you can really get on the good side of that person.

There are different methods that you can use in order to commit someone's name to memory. You can repeat the name a few times in that conversation to get it to stick. You can use your imagination and association to help you to remember the name. The more creative that you can get with these remembering devices, the easier it is going to be to remember that name, and the better impression that you are going to give to that person if you succeed.

If you ever need to express some of your own opinions when you are talking to another person, make sure that you do this in a respectful way. While you don't want to have your views come across as though they are superior to what anyone else thinks, you can still voice your opinion and share your views. It is important to be authentic and just because you might have different views about a certain topic of discussion, it doesn't mean that you are going to lose your likeability in the process.

You can disagree with the opinions of others, but you need to do this in a manner that is polite, one that allows you to talk about your own thoughts but shows that you are fair and also value the opinion of that other person.

If you do both disagree on a point, you can stop the conversation and politely ask the other person to explain why they think the way that they do. This is going to show the other person that you are interested in hearing more about what they think, and then they will be more receptive to the things that you are going to say about your own opinion on the matter.

Refine your appearance

While it may seem a little bit shallow, one of the big things that will determine if someone likes you or not, is your appearance. The way you look will give someone a snap judgement of you, and it might influence how receptive they are to you when you first meet. If you show up in sweat pants or old clothes and don't take a bath or a shower for many days, then this sends the message that you don't care about yourself, and the opinion of a stranger meeting you for the first time you is most likely going to be low. But if you take care with your appearance and work to make yourself look good, then you will find that it is easier to make a good impression that will really make a difference.

There are a few things that you can do to make this happen. First, show some pride in your own personal style. Your clothing is going to be one of the first things that people notice when they see you. Having your own style, one that is unique and that shows that you take pride in your appearance, will prove to others that you have confidence in yourself, and then they will have confidence in you as well.

Next, you need to make sure that you are maintaining your own personal hygiene. You can have the best personality in the world, but if you smell bad or don't look like you maintain your hygiene, others are not going to want to be near you. If your goal is to become more likeable, then you should make it a habit to groom yourself each day.

This can include showering regularly, applying anti-perspirant, and washing your hands.

Oral hygiene is important here as well. To make sure that people are encouraged to talk to you, it is important to take two minutes each day to brush your teeth, two times a day or more, to help remove the bacteria that is there, to make your breath smell better, and to keep those pearly whites looking great when you smile. Take the time to replace your toothbrush at least four times a year to keep it healthy.

Oral hygiene doesn't stop with brushing your teeth. For example, you can also take some time to floss each day, or use some chap stick on dry lips on a regular basis, especially if you are in the colder months.

And finally, make sure that you are careful with the makeup that you are using. You can use it in order to enhance your own appearance and to make sure that the best parts of your face will be highlighted, but you don't want to overdo it. Keep the makeup to a minimum, rather than caking it on, to help you appear more natural and to make others feel more comfortable around you.

You will be amazed at some of the things that you can get to happen, and how much easier it is to feel confident, when you feel that you are more likeable to the other people around you. They are more likely to want to come over and talk to you, more likely to listen to the things that you say and to ask questions, and more likely to want to be your friend, even if you are a very shy introvert. Taking care to follow these tips to be more confident and likeable, can really make a difference in improving small talk and other communication techniques.

Chapter 10: How to Start and Build Up Relationships as an Introvert

As an introvert, you may find that making new friends is not always as easy as it can be for others. Introverts like to go more for quality when picking out their friends, rather than quantity. So, while some people are interested in going all out and having as many friends as possible, introverts tend to be more selective and picky, and will only choose friends that really understand them, who share the same interests, and who are willing to accept them as they are.

If an introvert is not able to share their innermost thoughts, secrets, and dreams with another person, then they are never really going to consider that other person their friend. They may see this person as a nice acquaintance, or someone they like a lot, but not really a true friend. Because of this desire for more depth and quality in their friendships, the introvert is perfectly fine having just one or two friends.

Of course, this doesn't mean that introverts aren't allowed to have a large number of friends if they want. Some introverts are more sociable and thrive with a larger number of friends. But this doesn't mean that they are going to run out and get more friends just to say that they have them.

However, introverts will often find that it is harder for them to develop the high-quality friendships that they are looking for. They have trouble when it comes to reaching out to new people, and even when they do, it is hard for them to find someone they "click" with.

The issue here is that all humans, whether they are introverts or extroverts, are made to be in society and to seek out relationships. In fact, there are many studies out there that show that being social and having close relationships with others increases the mental and physical health of the individual, along with their overall happiness. But a lack of close friendships, and some of the isolation that comes with this, can have the exact opposite effect.

Despite the belief that most introverts don't even like other people, these individuals need human connection, just like everyone else does. But they are going to have some different needs when it comes to their relationships.

A good way to think about the emotional needs of an introvert, compared to an extrovert, is that they are fine having other people around and in the same house, but they don't want a lot of people in the same room as them all the time. They are fine with people, but they get energy from spending time on their own, without other people being on top of them.

However, the world around them is not always going to be the most conducive to this ideal. The world is often going to be loud and in-their-face—and sitting next to someone in silence isn't really going to create much of a lasting friendship. It is important to remember that introverts are just as able to create some of the human connections that they need, but sometimes they need to step away from their own comfort zones in order to make this happen.

There are some things that you can do in order to make it easier to find friends, even when you are an introvert. It actually isn't as hard as you may think.

If you don't have the energy to reach out to others, find ways to draw them to you

As an introvert, there are going to be times when you are too worn out, or too uncomfortable, to go around and try to make small talk to find new friends. You may get into a room full of people, and just want to scurry the other way. This is fine. It is okay to not always have the energy that is needed to be overly social and to be out there chasing down others and trying to do all the work to form the connections you need.

This doesn't mean that you should give up. It just means that you should find other ways to get this done. One method that can be just as effective, if not better, is to find a way to draw others to come to you, rather than you going to them. The idea of a smile can go a long way here too.

No matter what mood you are in, no matter how tired you are, and no matter what circumstances are going on around you ahead of time, make sure that your ultimate goal is to smile as much as possible.

Let's say that you are at a party and you see someone else walk into the room. If you make eye contact with them and smile at them, they are going to notice you, and maybe even come over to talk. That is, if they are interested in making a connection themselves. If they don't come over, then you can just keep going with the things you were doing before. If they do come over, you have created a friendly start to meeting someone new, and all you had to do was smile. You can greet them warmly and they will most likely start a conversation and try to keep it going, and you can just go along for the ride.

It isn't always your job to charm others

Shy introverts can feel a lot of pressure in social settings to be outgoing, vivacious, and charming, fearing that there is no way that another person will ever like them or become their friend. When they try to be charming or outgoing, it usually doesn't go all that well.

Often, they will struggle and get their words jumbled, or get lots of nervous laughter, and the situation just gets more uncomfortable for them as it goes on.

The thing to remember here is that there isn't really a rule in place that says you absolutely need to be a charmer to have any hope of making connections. Instead of working so much on charming others, or trying to behave the way that an extrovert would, work on being confident in yourself. Learn how to be self-assured in the things that you appreciate and stand for; for the interests and values that you have; and in who you are.

There is nothing wrong with being "the quiet one" when out in a social setting. Sure, there is a lot of push back in our world against this, where people think that you need to be outgoing and act a certain way, but this just isn't the way that most introverts work.

When you are ready to reach out to another person, then go ahead and do it. If you don't, then don't pressure yourself. If someone does start to approach you, don't feel nervous. If you feel confidence in who you are as a person, and your innate likeability, then it doesn't matter what the other person thinks of you, or if there are awkward moments in your conversation. The more comfortable you are with not being the life of the party, and the less you try to change your personality, the more likely it is that you can actually start to enjoy yourself and attract the kind of people and friendships that will be best for you.

It is fine to be vulnerable on occasion

For many introverts, it is sometimes hard to be vulnerable. Many of these individuals like to keep to themselves, and they strive to showcase a perfect persona to everyone they come across. But when building friendships, think of these words from C.S. Lewis: "Friendship is born at the moment when one person says to another: 'What! You too? I thought I was the only one...'" This moment is not going to happen between you and another person unless you can be courageous enough to open yourself up.

The deeper that you are willing and able to go into these new friendships, the more meaning there is going to be behind them. Building up to revealing a healthy amount of vulnerability is going to need to start somewhere. Why can't it start with you? Showing someone else that you are willing to be honest and open gives them permission to be honest and open as well. You can both feed off each other in this way, in a cycle that will create a deeper bond than before.

There are a lot of ways that you can show some vulnerability to another person. When you are meeting someone new, you can keep it simple. You don't have to introduce yourself and then start talking about all your biggest fears in the first five minutes. Some examples of how to initially show some vulnerability could include the following admissions:

> 1. "I really wish that there were some people I knew at this gathering."
> 2. "Do you know any good ice breakers? I've never been really good at them."
> 3. "I don't know about you, but I really am not a fan of these kinds of big parties."

After you have had a chance to talk with someone for a while, or maybe met up with them more than once, it is time to build up the relationship some more. The way that you show more vulnerability will change as the relationship develops. Some examples of things that you can say to show your vulnerability as you are starting to build up these new relationships, include:

> 1. "I start to feel pretty anxious when I get to a new class."
> 2. "I like hanging out with you."
> 3. "I'm having some trouble with [fill in the problem here]. Can I have a few minutes to vent to you?"
> 4. "I really appreciate the way that you have been supporting me."

It is so important to be vulnerable with another person if you are going to be friends. Friends should be those people who you feel comfortable to share personal life with. If you just want to work on outward appearances forever and never really dig into any of the things that matter to you, then you are just acquaintances. But when you open up and allow yourself to be vulnerable a little bit, then you are going to find that deeper bonds can begin to form.

Seek out other introverts like yourself

There is nothing wrong with picking out an extrovert to be your friend. They may help to get you out more socially and to experience different things in life, and they can be a lot of fun. This piece of advice isn't telling you to completely avoid making friends with extroverts. If you feel a connection with them, go for it.

But if all of your friends are extroverts, then it can sometimes be emotionally draining, since they will want to go out and be social all the time, while you crave some peace and quiet in your own home.

As an introvert, it is sometimes better for most of your friends to be introverts, and for you to look out for other introverts to spend time with. Any time that you do go out in a social setting, whether it is to a party, to a camp, or to school, etc. your goal should be to search out other introverts like yourself, who will likely understand you better and give you the space that you need.

There are a lot of benefits to picking out introverts as your friends. They aren't going to pressure you to change the way that you think or your personality. They won't try to turn you into a vivacious human when you aren't. So, how do you find these people? Look around the room and see if there is anyone who is quietly hanging out along the edges. Then you can make the first move and go and talk to them. It could be the start of a great new friendship.

Figure out the love language of the other person, and then share what yours is

Although the Five Love Languages are often geared towards relationships that are more romantic, they can be used in many other situations as well. Partners have used them to help understand each other better. Parents have used them to help understand their children and how to better raise them. And you can even use these love languages to deepen the friendships that you have.

There are some simple tests that you can take to figure out what your love language is, and then you can learn a bit more about the others as well. Not everyone is going to have the same love language as you. By assuming that everyone sees things the way that you do, you miss out on appreciating how unique each individual is, which can lead to disagreements and make it harder to form the deep connections that are needed.

There are five of these love languages to watch out for, and they include: physical touch; acts of service; words of affirmation; gifts; and quality time. We often find that we will give out love the same way that we want to receive it. But if the other person we are trying to connect with has a different love language, the desired effect is not going to be received.

For example, if "acts of service" is your love language, you may be more likely to run errands for the other person, help them clean up, or make them dinner. But if their love language is "physical touch", then there can be a disconnect. This doesn't mean that they won't appreciate the things that you do, it just won't lead to a deep connection. You need to meet them where their love language is, and they have to meet you where your love language is, in order to form those great connections.

The first step is to know your love language. Take a look at the five options listed above and see if any of them sticks out for you when it comes to how you react to other people and what behavior you appreciate the most from others. If you are uncertain, you can consider working with an online test to help you out. Once you know what your own love language is, you can then focus on the love language of those around you, making it easier for you to connect in a better and more effective, manner.

Hold out for the true connections, and don't try to settle

This is something that is going to come naturally for a lot of introverts, but it is never something that hurts to be reminded about. There is nothing quite like the moment of two souls meeting. You shouldn't just rush out and make friends with the first person you run across, unless you and that person are really able to click, and you feel a deeper connection with them. Hold out for a bit and see if you can find someone who really completes you, who really "gets" you, rather than just jumping on the first friendship opportunity that you find.

As an introvert, it is a good idea to hold out for a good friend. Hold out for someone who is going to make you feel safe and comfortable right away. Hold out for someone you feel that you can talk to about anything, without having to worry about them judging you. Hold out for someone who is able to make you happy.

It can take many introverts some time to open themselves up to others, because they are already so aware of their own internal lives. The good thing about this is that many times, they are able to get a quick sense about whether they connect with someone or not.

Introverts can get impatient when they aren't able to make those deep connections quickly. But remember that it is always worth it to hold out for that one in a million friend.

Be intentional

As an introvert, you are going to need to take some extra steps and precautions to ensure that you can reach out to other people. Many introverts may find that it is easy to get caught up in their own world, and then not talk to others for a long period of time. It may feel like they are ignoring other people, or that they don't really care, but in reality, they may lose sight of things or not even think about it.

It is important that you don't fall into this trap. You have to check in with your friends often, and this is going to get even more important the older that you get. Of course, it is also something that is going to get quite a bit harder—especially if you keep saying, "We should get together…" but then don't make it a priority as time goes by. Unfortunately, for many friendships, especially when they involve introverts, this can easily happen.

However, you will find that a little effort is going to go a long way. You don't have to make it something big or do a grand gesture each time you catch up. A simple text message to check in with the other person, a Skype or phone call, or a meetup or event planned in advance can all help you to maintain your friendships better, even when you are dealing with being separated by time or space.

It is going to take some work to make your friendships last. You need to make sure that you are intentional in setting up time to prioritize other people, even when it feels impossible or exhausting. When you are able to do this, you will find that it leads to relationships that are deeper and more meaningful, and this can do so much good for your mental, emotional, and physical wellbeing.

Chapter 11: Other Ways to Increase Your Communication Skills

There are so many ways that we can communicate with the world around us. We can write letters, send out emails, send out texts, and talk to others on the phone or in person. There is even a whole part of communication that is nonverbal and doesn't include any words at all. It is so important, whether you are an introvert or an extrovert, to learn how to communicate with those around you, whether by engaging in small talk, business talk, or deeper conversations.

In this chapter, we are going to look at some of the other things that you can do in order to increase your own communication skills. Strong communication skills can benefit you in a wide variety of situations, and some of the things that you can do to increase your communication skills and make them better include the following:

Get rid of any conversation fillers that aren't necessary

The um's and ah's may be a normal part of the way that you talk, but they aren't going to do that much to improve your speech or the way that your everyday conversations go. You need to find ways to cut them out as much as possible. This will help you to become more persuasive, to make you appear and feel more confident, and can really help the flow of the conversation.

But how do you work to break this habit, one that has most likely been formed many years ago? One way that you can do this is to start keeping a rolling tally of when you say any filler words—anything like ah, um, like, or any other word that really has no meaning. Once you see just how many times you are saying these words in each conversation, you will be amazed and motivated to focus on and improve the problem.

There are also a few other things that you can do to help this situation. Sometimes just finding ways to relax when you are in the middle of a conversation can make a difference. When you are tense and nervous, which can often happen when a shy introvert gets out in a public setting and engages in small talk, those filler sounds and words are going to be more likely. Simply taking some steps, like removing your hands from your pockets and taking some pauses before you speak, can really cut down on these.

Often, we will start to rush through some of the sentences and words that we want to say. We are worried about having any pauses in the conversation. The truth is that those silences are always going to seem more awkward to us, but often the other person isn't even going to notice. It is much better to have a few seconds of pause so you can think through what you are going to say next, rather than slowing down your thoughts and making it sound jarring as you add in those unnecessary filler words.

Consider having a script to help with the small talk

Small talk may sound pretty simple in theory, but in reality, it is an art form that a lot of people struggle with. It is important to be as prepared as possible. And for some introverts, having a small script with ideas and suggestions can be the answer to this problem.

The FORD method can be the right option to help you out. FORD stands for family, occupation, recreation, and dreams. This is a good way to remember a few topics that you are able to discuss with another person. Just thinking of those words may be enough to help push you forward to having a new topic to talk about. You can also use these to help you turn awkward small talk into a better conversation as you share information that could help you and the other person find some common ground with each other.

You can also think about a few things that you would say for each topic of family, occupation, recreation and dreams. You don't want to go into any conversation and have the whole thing scripted out. This will be painfully obvious to the other person and is going to turn them off of you pretty early on. But when you do just enough to help you get started, and then you just let the conversation go its natural course, you will be amazed at how much easier it is to talk with anyone, whether you have known them for a long time or just met.

Ask lots of questions, and try repeating what the other person says

This is not a suggestion to just parrot another person and not bring anything to the table conversationally. And it also isn't about just asking question after question without talking about yourself ever. But it is a good way to get the other person talking and to ensure that you keep the conversation going without too many awkward pauses or other issues.

No doubt there have been times that, no matter how hard you tried, you drifted off when someone else was talking and missed out on what they were saying. This has happened to all of us at some point—humans are distractible creatures. Or on other occasions, perhaps you were paying attention, but misheard what another person said.

Asking questions during a conversation, and stopping at times to repeat what that other person has said can help to clarify anything that may seem confusing, and can help you stay in the moment and keep up with the conversation.

Try not to make this seem annoying though, by constantly just repeating everything they are saying and not adding anything yourself. But if you find a way to repeat some of the words in your follow up sentence, this can really help you to remember what was going on during the conversation.

This can also help you to fill up any of the awkward silences that naturally show up when you are using small talk. Instead of trying to stir up a conversation with all of the usual and boring topics, such as how the weather has been, you can ask some interesting questions of the other person to get them talking. Then, when they provide you with some answers, you can work on engaging with those answers. Remember, it is always more important in small talk for you to be interested in the other person, more than being interesting to them.

Find ways to tailor your message to the audience

The best communicators out there are the ones that can adjust how they talk and the message that they are discussing based on who they are talking to.

You may already be doing this without even realizing it. Think about it this way, do you use the same tone, the same communication style, or even the same topics, when you are talking to your co-workers compared to talking to your family? Do you talk to your friends, teachers, boss, and people you just met in the same manner as each other? Probably not.

When you are ready to engage in small talk, try to remember the perspective of the other person, and the best way to approach or get through to them. For example, if you are talking to your boss at work, you will need to keep things professional, so it would not be appropriate to tell them that you are feeling tired and unproductive because you are hungover from the night before. However, if you are with a close friend, you might feel more relaxed, and even hug them, before you ask for an update on a personal matter.

Tailoring your message to your audience can help you to communicate a bit easier. You can keep in mind the context of your relationship, and think of some things that they enjoy, or where they work and what they do in their free time, or even about their personal life if you know them, and you will find plenty of topics that can help you out with this approach.

Be brief and specific

Small talk can sometimes lead to deeper conversations, but often this is just a time to quickly catch up. It is always a good idea to be specific and brief, rather than going on about a topic that no one is interested in.

The acronym BRIEF—background, reason, information, end, and follow up—can be used to help with this. Following this formula helps you to be succinct and to keep conversations relevant, by giving some quick context, or background information, followed by the reason that you've brought up a particular topic now. Then make sure to highlight the key information that you want to share, before wrapping it up. Finally, you can follow up by considering any questions that might crop afterwards. This is great to remember when it comes to sending emails and written correspondence but using BRIEF to be clear and concise can also work to prevent boredom when dealing with verbal communication as well.

Up the level of empathy that you provide

Always remember that communication is a two-way street. You should never be the only one who is talking the whole time, and you should also never just be listening the whole time. There needs to be some talking and some listening on both sides to ensure that the conversation keeps going, and that no one feels like they are either being ignored or doing all the work.

In addition to this, you may find that showing some empathy is going to make a big difference as well. It can help you to relate to the other person and figure out how to connect on a deeper level. It doesn't mean you need to be a people pleaser who only ever says what you think others want to hear, but it does mean that you will have a sense of how a person might be feeling when you discuss a certain topic. This can also help to avoid seeming awkward and insensitive by accidentally bulldozing over the other person's feelings, because you lack the ability to recognize them or to put yourself in the other person's shoes.

You can develop empathy with anyone; you don't have to be close to them. Developing empathy is going to help you to get a better understanding of everything that the other person is saying, even some of the unspoken parts. For example, if your friend tells you that they are excited that their child has gotten his first tooth, you might notice that while they are smiling when they say this, they also look very tired and have low energy. You can empathize with them by saying something like: "Wow, that's great! And you must also be happy to get some more sleep now that he isn't teething and in so much pain." It will be a relief for the proud parent to acknowledge that yes, they are also exhausted and hoping for a more settled night now that their son's tooth is finally out. In addition to forming a deeper connection with that person, empathy can also help you to respond more effectively in all of your communications with others.

Realize the importance of body language

Body language is a big part of communication, and yet it is something that too many people don't even pay conscious attention to in the first place. In many cases, it is going to be more accurate to assess what a person feels and means from their body language, than the words that are used. If someone says: "I am happy", but they are standing up tall and tense, with an angry tone and their fists clenched, then it is likely that they are actually angry rather than happy. But we had to look at the body language to figure this out.

The old saying, "Actions speak louder than words", is true, and sometimes it is possible for individuals to communicate a lot of different things without having to utter a single word. For example, how often have you been able to shrug your shoulders and—without saying a word—convey that you don't know the answer to something? Or, how many times have you simply raised your eyebrows, to convey that you can't believe what the other person has just said? Likewise, how many times have you gestured your hands with the palms up in front of you to suggest: "I don't know what else to say"?

There are also times when body language can be used in order to help reinforce some of the words that we are saying. We might get excited about something and move our hands around to show this. Or we might hunch our shoulders and have a sad tone when we are talking about something that is bringing us down.

In addition, paying attention to the body language that someone else is sending out is going to help us figure out whether that other person is telling us the truth, or if they are outright lying or just leaving something out of the equation. There are quite a few signs that will show when a person is lying. For example, they may clear their throat, stammer or change the pitch of their voice, or stall so that they can think about another plausible explanation. They may tap their foot, put their hands on their face, blush, or even raise their shoulders to show that they are uncomfortable, since they aren't telling the truth.

This is just one example of how you can use body language to figure out what the other person is really thinking or feeling. You can tell when someone is anxious, when they are angry, when they are happy and excited, or even when they are sad, based more on the body language cues that they send out than on the words that they say.

Another example is if an employee tells their boss that they would be more than happy to take on a new account, but their body language cues show that they really aren't happy about taking on that extra work at all, and they would rather be doing something else.

If the management isn't paying attention, they are going to just listen to the words and assume the employee will take on the work with no problems. But when the leadership and the managers really start to pay attention to the nonverbal cues that the employee is sending out, they will realize that they should try to find someone else to handle the assignment. The employee may not want to disappoint their boss, so they choose to say "yes", even though their heart is not really that into it.

Body language can be used in a job interview in many cases. If the body language of a particular application shows that they are really at ease with the subject matter, and they are good at conveying confidence during the interview questions, then there is a higher chance that this individual is going to get the job, especially if the job market is tough. On the other hand, if the applicant goes into the interview with a look of being uncomfortable or appears like they are not in control, these are traits that will turn the interviewer off and can harm your chances of getting the job.

Body language can also be important when it comes to making friendships. No one wants to have a full conversation with another person and feel like they are being blown off or not paid any attention to.

So, how do you know whether or not someone is paying attention or if they really care about what you have to say? If the other person is leaning forward—into that conversation rather than away from it—this indicates an interest in the topic. Listening to the other person and making eye contact can show interest as well. These are signs that you can look for when you are talking to someone else, and that you can use when you are also trying to convey interest.

There are a lot of different types of body language that you can pay attention to in order to figure out whether or not someone is actually saying what the words are saying. Some different aspects of body language that you should pay attention to include:

> 1. **Eye movement and contact:** When you are trying to work with good communication and you want to make sure that your body language is saying the things that you want it to, you must make sure to pay attention to eye movement and eye contact. When talking to someone else, maintain eye contact with them, and don't let your eyes wander off. If you

let this happen, you are showing the other person that you are bored or that there are other things that are more important and worthy of your attention. This can be seen as rude and can make it hard to create those deeper connections that you are socializing and starting small talk to find.

2. **Posture:** Posture is another determinant that you need to look at to figure out if someone means the words that they are saying, and if you are getting the whole story from them. Someone who is comfortable and confident is going to stand up with good posture. They will stand up straight and tall, have a smile on their face, and will keep good eye contact throughout the whole conversation. Someone who isn't confident—and who maybe isn't enjoying the conversation—will slouch a bit, have trouble keeping eye contact, and will maybe even turn their body away from you in an attempt to walk away.

3. **Where the hands go:** The hands will provide a big clue to how the other person is feeling or what they are thinking. If they have their arms folded across their chest, this can indicate that they are defensive or uncomfortable in the situation. But if their hands are moving around and excited, it could show that they are really animated by the subject at hand.

Hand placement can also indicate whether they are confident, comfortable, or tense. If the other person appears to be tense when they are around you, then it may be a sign that you are doing or saying something that makes them this way, or maybe you both aren't clicking. Sometimes you can figure out why they are so tense based on what they are saying. For example, if they are talking about a bad week at work, that could possibly be why their shoulders are all tense. But in other cases, it may be more of a sign that something is wrong with the conversation or how they feel, and it may be time to give them a break and find someone else to talk with.

4. **Tone of voice:** The tone of voice that the other person uses is going to reveal a lot when it comes to figuring out what they really mean. The words that someone repeats and their tone of voice can reveal completely different ideas in some cases. If you are uncertain about what the other person means, then try to pay attention to their tone of voice and see if this offers some clues.

5. **How close they stand:** You don't want someone to be so close to you that it makes you feel uncomfortable. But you also don't want them so far away that you almost have to scream in order to have a conversation, especially in a crowded space. The body position of the other person can indicate how comfortable they are with you. If you notice that someone is standing further away, or they seem to be inching themselves a bit away from you as you talk, this can indicate that they aren't comfortable being around you at the time, or that they need to be somewhere else. But if the person is faced towards you and keeps a steady distance that is close enough for comfort, then it is a good sign that they enjoy spending time with you and want to keep the conversation going.

There are so many different aspects that can come with good communication when you are talking to another person. You have to worry about how your body language is working, you have to pay attention to the other person and not always be thinking about the things that you are going to say next, and you have to come up with good topics that can keep the conversation going. But if you are able to remember a few of these tips and the other tips we have talked about, you will find that small talk is easier than you think, and it won't take long until you start to make the meaningful connections that you are looking for.

Chapter 12: Tips to Help You Develop Your Social Skills

If you feel like you are always that one awkward guest at social events, or like you consistently struggle to get into new conversations because you are shy, then it is possible that this negative self-talk is affecting your career and social life. By improving your social skills, you will begin to feel more comfortable no matter the social situation, you will make new friends and have more fun when you go out—even when you are an introvert.

Start acting like a social person

This can be hard. You may find that instead of being out and talking to people all the time, you would rather head home instead. But over time, socializing will get easier.

This doesn't mean that you have to go and change your whole personality. There are so many great things about being an introvert, but if you can do a bit of acting and behave a little more social when you go out, even when you don't feel it, you may find that small talk and joining in on conversations can start to feel more natural. Don't allow anxiety or shyness to get in the way and make things more difficult. It is up to you to make the decision to talk to new people, and to start these conversations, even when you feel a bit nervous about it.

It is fine to start out small

As an introvert, you probably don't want to spend all your free time going to parties or putting yourself in a ton of social situations. Introverts can sometimes get nervous just seeing their calendar fill up for the month. They want to be able to sit back and enjoy some things, and sometimes after a long week at work, they would like to have a few nights off at home to be alone and to recharge before hitting the social scene again.

If going out each night to a party or spending a lot of time out in a crowd seems overwhelming to you, it is fine to start out small. You should still work your way up to being more social and going out at least occasionally. But a "slow and steady" approach can definitely get you there as well.

One way to start small, is to just say "Thank you" to the grocery store clerk the next time you go shopping. Then, after a few times of this, start making some small talk by mentioning the weather, or asking about the person's family, or how they are doing in school. This can help you get some more practice with small talk and can make it easier to engage in conversation with others when you do go out in more social settings.

It is easier to get others to talk about themselves

Many introverts find that it is uncomfortable to talk about themselves when they are with others. They feel that doing this makes them seem like they are bragging or puts the spotlight on them. They would much rather let the other person do most of the talking, and let the other person talk about themselves, while they spend the time asking lots of questions.

The good news is that you can easily turn the conversation around. In fact, you will find that many of the other people that you meet are going to really love talking about themselves. When they find an ear that is ready to listen, they will often just go on and on, and soon you will have made a good ally, and all you needed to do was ask questions and show your interest in that other person.

How do you get this all started? Simply ask a question about the other person. This can be about their family, about their hobbies, or about their career. Just keep asking questions, interjecting with some of your own information when asked, and otherwise just let the other person keep going. Encourage others to talk so that you won't have to be the one who is making all the idle chit-chat all the time.

To help with this, make sure that you are asking open-ended questions, which require more than a yes or a no answer from the other person. If you simply ask closed-ended questions, then you will get very short answers and most likely run out of conversation really quickly.

Also, if the other person does ask you some questions, try to give a full answer. Don't respond with only a "Yes" or "No", even if the question is a little bit closed ended. Doing this will shut down the effort that the other person has made, and they may feel like you don't want to keep the conversation going. Instead, choose to expand on any question that they ask, allowing both you and the other person to feed off each other.

Create goals for yourself

There are many different goals that you can set yourself in order to get the most out of your social improvement. You can choose to open your front door when someone rings the bell and talk with them for a few minutes. You can agree to sign up for a class or a workshop, and then make it your aim to talk to someone at each class. You can start attending a social activity in the community and go to regular meetings, where you will get to know other locals.

When you pick out goals, you must go with ones that will challenge you a bit, that will push you out of your comfort zone, but which won't be so difficult that you aren't able to reach them. Establish a goal and then pick out the right strategies that will help you to attain it, so you end up improving your social life, step-by-step.

Start out with one goal at a time when you are doing this, so that you don't take on too much at once. Pick one of the goals above, or a different social goal that appeals to you, and then build up from there. This way, you can work off the success that you see from achieving the first goal, and build confidence and momentum to attempt the second goal, and so on.

Remember to compliment others

Compliments are going to be your best friend. They don't take long to come up with, and they will make the other person feel amazing. It is such a simple way to get on the good side of another person, and you will find that the conversation will flow much more freely as a result.

Compliments are one of the best ways for you to open the door to a new conversation. You can offer one of your co-workers a compliment on how hard they worked on the presentation they just gave. You can compliment a friend on their new promotion, or a neighbor for getting a new car. There is always something that you can praise another person for, even if it is as simple as pointing out that you like their jacket, and asking where they got it from.

Compliments should show others that you are friendly. Friendly people are willing to give out compliments, whether they know the person well or not, and leading the discussion with a compliment, or finding another natural place to add it in, can go a long way.

Try it the next time that you meet someone new. Take a few seconds while you are being introduced to find something about that person that you can praise them on. You can choose their outfit, their shoes, their handshake, their hair, or something else. The compliment doesn't have to be big, but it shows that you are really noticing the other person and helps draw them to you.

Keep yourself up to date on any current events

One of the hardest things that you have to deal with when working on small talk, is finding topics to discuss with other people. There are many different topics you can discuss with another person, including friends, family, hobbies, career, interests, and current events.

Current events, as long as they are not too controversial, can be a great topic to bring up, and can lead to a longer conversation as you and the other person go back and forth on the different stories in the news that you have read about. The best way to take advantage of this is to keep up to date on all the news stories and current trends that you can find, which will help you to have something to talk about on any occasion. For example, you can look online, watch the news, and read magazines to help you out.

The important thing is to avoid any topic that is too controversial, including religion and politics. You don't want to ruin a potential friendship just because you decided to bring up politics in the first few minutes of meeting someone new. But do take the time to talk about any of the other current events and news stories that may be of interest.

Practice makes perfect

Practice is one of the best ways to help you improve your social skills. If you just read through this guidebook, but never get out in a social situation to use these suggestions, then they are just theories and you will never get better. You have to put yourself in social situations to help you get in some practice to see the progress that you want to make.

Anyone, including a shy introvert, can learn how to improve their social skills. It can take time, and you may make mistakes along the way, but it is going to be so worth it in the long run. The more that you can get out and the longer you practice, the better you will get at this endeavor.

Try getting out just a few times a month, and build up from there

For an introvert, it can sometimes be difficult to get yourself out there and into social situations. Sometimes just going to work and to the store throughout the week is enough to exhaust you. But if you want to work on your social skills, you need to avoid making excuses, and put yourself in social situations.

Likewise, if you are shy, you can also struggle to get out and meet people, but this is because you don't know how to express yourself and are afraid of being embarrassed or rejected. To gain confidence and get around this fear, while learning to communicate effectively, it is also important to get out and expose yourself more socially.

You don't have to go out every night of the week. You just need to get out a little more than usual. Even just adding one or two social events to your calendar a month can make a big difference in how much you work on your social skills. And the more you get out there, the more comfortable you will feel. In fact, you may even find that social activities, when limited and on your own terms, can be more enjoyable.

You get the freedom to pick out what social events you would like to attend, like a reading club at the library, or out with a few friends to get coffee. You can go to a meeting in the civic center of your town or just go out to a restaurant with your partner, instead of getting food delivered to your home. This all helps you to get out of the house, talk to different people, and to expand your comfort zone a little bit. The rest of the nights of the month can be reserved for going home and recharging at your own pace.

Identify and then replace any of the negative thoughts that you have

Many people who struggle with small talk and social interactions may also have a lot of negative thoughts about themselves as a result of this. This is particularly true if the person has difficulty because of intense shyness or social anxiety, and they may assume that no one likes them, that they are going to say something "stupid", or that they will just end up embarrassing themselves. The biggest problem with constantly entertaining these ideas is that they can become a self-fulfilling prophecy.

For example, it is harmful to tell yourself: "I'm so awkward, if I go to the party, no one will want to talk to me or I will just end up embarrassing myself." Because of these negative thoughts and the desire to avoid being embarrassed, you may just sit in the corner alone for the whole party. Then, when you leave, you will think that it must be true that you are too awkward, because no one talked to you all night.

If you want to get better at your social skills and learn how to communicate well with others, you need to learn how to get rid of these unhealthy thinking patterns. Start by identifying the negative thoughts that are dragging you down. Once you have found those, you can work on replacing them with other more positive and realistic thoughts, which will help to build your confidence instead.

By making these changes, you get to control your own destiny. Instead of thinking that you are awkward and certain to make mistakes, you can start out with a little pep talk to get through each social situation. For example, the next time that you go out to a social event, start out by telling yourself "I can make friendly conversation and I can meet new people."

It is so important that you don't allow yourself to dwell on unproductive thoughts that work against you and the change you want to inspire in your life. If a thought makes you feel bad about yourself, or keeps you from socializing with others, then it is destructive and should be challenged.

Having a good set of social skills is so essential when it comes to being an effective communicator. Great social skills are not easy, and everyone experiences awkwardness sometimes. You have to keep trying and keep putting yourself out there, even if you do happen to fail. You will get better over time, and these social skills can serve you well for your whole life. It's never too late to start trying some of these suggestions to help you change the way you see yourself, as you learn to communicate with ease.

Conclusion

Thank you for making it through to the end of *Small Talk: A Shy Introverts Guide to Being More Likeable and Building Better Relationships, Even If You Have Social Anxiety, Including Conversation Starters and Tips for Improving Your Social Skills*. Let's hope it was informative and able to provide you with all of the tools you need to achieve your goals—whatever they may be.

The next step is to start putting some of these tips and tricks to good use and see what a difference they can make in your communication skills with others. As a shy introvert, it can sometimes be difficult to talk with others and form some of the meaningful connections that you are looking for. You may want to make friends, but socializing can exhaust you, which makes it unappealing to go out, and if you are also shy, your fear can hold you hostage when you really want to be out and making friends. You do need to take the time to recharge your batteries before social encounters, which means that any socialization you do participate in needs to count, but you also need to build up the skills and ability to overcome your fears and negative self-talk as well.

Small talk may not be something that introverts really enjoy doing, but it is something that forms a basis for all great relationships. This guidebook has all the tips that you need to really become an expert at small talk, and to get it to work for you. By applying the principles explained in this book, you can take control of your life and learn not only to communicate effectively, but to find joy in social interactions.

By the time that you are done implementing these suggestions, you will be an expert at small talk and be able to wow anyone at your next social gathering, even as a shy introvert.

Here's another book by Matt Holden that you might like

www.ingramcontent.com/pod-product-compliance
Lightning Source LLC
Chambersburg PA
CBHW020127130526
44591CB00032B/563